FOUND AT SEA

HOY

BROAD REACH

CLOSE REACH

FORCED GYBE

REEF

ROPE

HOUTON

CAVA

TACK

BEAM REACH

CLOSE HAULED

GRAEMSAY

FOUND AT SEA

The Expanded Log of the
'Arctic Whaler'
to overnight on Cava

Andrew Greig

Polygon

For Marsali Baxter, James Burgon, Andrew Glaister,
Mark Shiner and Chris Carver, who generously took me to sea.

All panel artworks by Mike McDonnell of Yell,
canoeist, islander, shantyman.

———————————————

This edition first published in paperback in Great Britain in 2013
by Polygon, an imprint of Birlinn Ltd
West Newington House,
10 Newington Road
Edinburgh EH9 1QS

www.polygonbooks.co.uk

ISBN: 978 1 84697 269 0

British Library Cataloguing-in-Publication Data
A catalogue record for this book is available on request from the British
Library

Design by James Hutcheson
Printed and bound by Bell & Bain Ltd, Glasgow

ACKNOWLEDGEMENTS

I am indebted to Mark Shiner – fine musician, luthier, skipper, pal – for many outings on the '*Arctic Whaler*' including the one mythed here. Also to John Glenday and Lesley Glaister for their helpful, perceptive readings of early drafts.

Details of the journey of Miss Woodham and Miss Peckham to Orkney, and of their remarkable lives on Fara then Cava, can be read in an interview with them for a Kirkwall Grammar School project, available in the Orkney Archive, Kirkwall. A photo of the house and another of the garden, taken by Willie Buchan in the 1970s, can be found on the Orkney Image Library website.

A one-off, script-in-hand performance of a theatrical version of '*Found At Sea*' was first performed at the Traverse Theatre, Edinburgh in August 2012, as part of '*Dream Plays*' series. Lewis Howden played Skip, Tam Dean Burn played Crew, directed by David Greig. (Banjo fills by AG).

To Lesley

THE WHALE THEMSELVES HARPOONED

BY MEMORY OF WARMTH BOOZE. HOME ANDREW GREIG

TALES OF ORKNEY MEN UNDER AURORA CHASING

VOYAGE
OUT

'And then went down to the ship,
Set keel to breaker, forth on the godly sea'

The 'Arctic Whaler'

(i) *The name*

Tales of Orkney men under aurora
chasing the whale, themselves harpooned
by memories of warmth, booze, home
- barbs of love won't pull loose -
made a fictive pub for Mackay Brown's
fine-crafted *'Hamnavoe'*;

the derelict store on Gareth's pier
was the set when the poem was filmed -
thereafter folk, as joke then custom
still cried it that; I knew it best
on those Hogmanays we thrashed
banjo, fiddles and guitar, huddled round the brazier
 (*'Into the fire of images / Gladly I put my hand'*)
by windowless window and doorless door;

then Mark's new boat needed a name:
this the declension by which she became

    the *'Arctic Whaler'*

(ii) *The specs*
'a sea-hawk, perched on its trailer by wind-swept Ness'

'Fine entry, shallow draft.
Raked transom,
generous turn of the bilge.
Hull shape: a squat wineglass.
Thus buoyant amidships, plenty freeboard
to comfort anxious crew, and wife.'

Plainly: a sixteen foot five
design by Bill Bailiff,
individual talent flourishing
in tradition of a North East workboat
for sail and oar:
                a stable tender
when whalers moved in for the kill,
or hauling cod from Tyne in summer,
haar a shroud over the shrouds.

If she went over,
two men could not right her.
'Fear not. She has hidden flotation chambers,
emergency flares in the lazarette - stern locker'.

Near-vertical stem, Bermudan rigged,
  good capacity, handles well
    singlehanded or with crew.
Ballast: cast-iron pigs
from the Town Hall's organ bellows.

Six foot three beam.
With centreboard raised, twelve inches draft.

From bronze fairlead to squat transom
what's not to love and find apt!
At all times when handling, remember
like a poem she's not a machine
                    but a *craft*.

(iii) *How she was re-made*

£850 in cash
raised by sale of the last dangerous toy
(a microlight, in Orkney - insanity!)
when Mark's first-born arrived.
Hull pulled from woodland mire,
mast shattered, where she'd sat
as though rehearsing a return to sea,
                  leaves waving all round
green as the channels off Wyre.

Refitted by hand, mindful
of canny Josh Slocum's *Spray*;
centreboard: a chunk of steel plate,
raised by home-made block and tackle;
mainsail from a Snipe, patched Thirties' jib.

All made good, winter through spring,
on downtime when firstborn slept
and his partner Kate carried the next,
each with their dream of launching;

suspecting themselves blessed,
growing the insatiable bairn,
comforting the comfortless bairn,

on funds raised by flogging
all non-essential goods,
they re-shaped a marriage –

means not of escape
but of prayer:
calm passage through turbulent weather.

STILL BEND WE
MUST OVER CHART COMPASS PROTRACTOR AND HAZARD
OUR BEST GUESS
IN THE MIDDLE OF LIFE HALF WAYS OVER
SCAPA FLOW: CHART 1:50 000
A.G.
M.S.

The Log (Skip)

Stromness low water 16.19
Wind SE backing ESE, force 4 freshening 5, gusting 6
Arctic Whaler: skipper M Shiner, crew AG

By faffing and luffing
lying off tidal Holms   wake-shaken (*Hamnavoe* ferry)
lee-stricken -

        finally past Ness on tide's turn
(partners and children already home).

Voyage windward, tide following.
Starboard tack, S. of *Cairston Roads* -
close reach, long haul to beam swell,
                rudder juddering...

        High freeboard, all sound.
Beat to *Clestrain* for protection
          port tack close-hauled fast running
Peter Skerry kept two points off.

Quit lee and shore for long reach to *Bring Deeps.*
    Real sea there
  swell running length of Scapa Flow
crew silent, ducking spray, sheets gripped in hand.
We leaned out wide then wider
  jib and main hard as board
    numb hand on kicking tiller
look to leeward where

home, wife, children, beloveds –
roller from windward slewed the *Whaler*.

(Half this chart's marked *comfort zone*,
the rest *danger*: we skid along
the raised crease between them)

– Eyes back to oncoming sea! –

A small emergency

In the middle of life, half way over
we find ourselves
                              scunnered
on a dark and gurly sea.

This was not the plan
but we are where we are
   – wherever that is!
Time for Skip and Crew
to plot anew.

It needs no wobbling compass
clutched in frozen mitt
to tell us we must adjust. These lumps
of water hurled over the freeboard
speak volumes: enough!
This was not the plan, to have children,
to not have children,
to be so far out of our depth? Tough.

A fresh tack, see where it takes us?
   Here comes the boom – duck!

Close-hauled, tight call? We'll never know.
The Arctic Whaler's an arrow
shot from wind's bow.
Skip and Crew glance, nod, grin,
tense and wide-awake as arctic terns
that know
            only as they dive
how it is they live.

Our GPS has gone down?
We'll do this by hand and eye.

Log (sea-stained)
Transit on Scad Head
18.10, tidal stream est. 3 knots,
bore off 4 points.
Crew learned the difference between 'heading' and 'bearing'.

     On starboard tack
      beam swell due S. off *Houton*
broken sea, boilerplates, white breaks, squall,
took in plenty water -
     tiller over hard
close-hauled we ran for *Green Head*,
not saying much .
      Feart? Oh,
      I suppose. Also wild,
wildly happy as we bawled *Shenandoah*
and bailed like billy-o.

Took a breather in lee of the Head,
             shared chocolate, welcome tea.

This Liquid Field (*off Green Head*)

To wake, work and sleep
  on land, shape life around

ten miles of known ground,
  find confirmation in its set embrace,

seemed right - the coastal Greigs
  all turned to face inland,

looked to end where they began.
  In short, we don't do sea.

Yet this liquid field,
  tide-ploughed, wind-harrowed,

reaped by men who often sank
  to fertilize it once again,

this shifting, pathless flux
  where our passage leaves no mark

as we juggle 'relative' and 'true' position,
  never quite going where we are pointing,

not in control yet self-correcting,
  holding to our course -

even as we lurch and reel
  and gunwhale shoulders wave aside,

in my late middle years
  travelling on water feels

more kin to *the way things are*.

(Canvas hardens, mast leans,
  we lean out the other side;

the tell-tale ribbons stream
  to mark our sail's set right.)

Life writing

In truth, Skip,
- I cleat the jib sheet,
lean on the kicking gunwhale, blow
warm these hands, examine close
the lines that forty years ago
a palmist claimed foretold
four children, an untroubled life, hah! –

of late I do not like my work.
Sitting in a shed inventing stuff
in your fifties
lacks dignity.

We were crossing *Bring Deeps*
and perhaps I spoke to take my mind off
all that lay below our keel.
Braced in the squall
we talked as men do not.

Hard to see
the true course we were taking
amid lurch and side-slip, slew, correction,
eyes fixed not on each other
but the oncoming commotion
as Mark spoke of his dead brother -

> The poison trail of inherited damage
> creeping up the arm,

love of music and love of junk
taking the road together,
great gigs
catastrophic gigs
cancelled gigs
busts, petty thefts, courtcases,
cleaning up, unexpected bail, then
the celebratory, accidental overdose -

from the start, Mark's own resolve
THIS ENDS HERE

– Thus, I guess, his Xian Faith
I appreciate but do not share,
my only anchor the kind
filled with the flux we move through,

and it came clear
our course is plotted
not by the life we've got
but the one we've vowed
to have not.

I'll have a No. 3 all over, ditch the beard.
A man entering his sixth decade
can't faff about. From here on
I'll play the only game in town.

Whatever that is, mate! –

We laughed, tacked hard to port, ducking the boom.
the Deeps being done, we sailed
into the open Flow
   as though abandoning our island destination.
   Out among the sink holes,
   we slewed through deep unease
   where different waters meet,
                and local events
     collude with swell raised
   by gales on the other side of the world.

We were close and not close
in position at tiller and amidships
wanting the squall over,
knowing this test is what we came for.
Faith and Doubt, our two-man crew
took turns to fling
overboard with plastic pail
the water deepening round our feet.

   The old salts weren't kidding –
   anything can happen out here!

Yet, truth having ventured
between us, the wind in our sails changed
and it felt right to convert again
headwind to fast running.

How she goes

And after all
how goes she *forward*
when the wind blows in our faces?

'Forces like clasping hands converge,'
Mark says. 'Sail's pushed sideways,
keel resists
       braced by liquid tonnage.
The outcome? As wet soap
squeezed in the hand,
             the boat squirts forward...'

And so we roll on
time and tide and wind against us
over wave after wave after wave;

we go on
      breathing
though every breath drives us back

and who does not awake
from time to time in broad daylight
among on-coming fellow citizens,
feels the pressure,
     then himself leaping
         forward and free?

Not Iron John

We are not here as Iron John –
nor womanless sad sacks.
Not Boy Racers in denial.

Speak for yourself, Crew!

Most of what's dear to us
is back on land.
At a certain age
    it's right to ask
what you gonna do with that.

Once in a while it becomes necessary
    to push the boat out
and take not so much a mini-break (yawn)
more a micro-Odyssey
to know what we mean by home.

Size does not seal the deal?

Nope -
to risk the body even a bittie
Whoah! That feels real,
though those who love us shake their head and sigh.

Just don't expect them to listen long
to our stories when we get home.

Best guess position

At sea
only one certainty
               NOW   HERE

Mark's hasty bearings insist
the *Arctic Whaler* sits
a hundred yards onshore

but we are not in that comforting
green field over there

but all at sea in this
toss, swell, break, flux,

surface stramash   and deep down
darkness:
         utter calm
sunk, a stone Buddha, at the bottom of all.

His paw white on tiller
mine clawed on sheets
close-hauled and cork-screwing
  we lean
              far out as we dare -

Hard crossing
        emerging island
headwind an ally
          fear our friend.

Tack

Not without dignity
work done twice

tack of the life
tack of the word

work in the hard
sail set to windward

doubled voyage
uncertain weather

landfall found if ever
second time round.

Event horizon

And we ourselves
    freed slaves, bound gods,
        unmade men, rulers of little craft,
       servants of the horizon

– that is to say, sailors -

happily or fearfully think of our lives
        going forward and clockwise
when we are pulled sideways and widdershins
by forces so pervasive
    we don't even see them.

Still bend we must
    over chart, compass, protractor,
      and hazard our best guess.

Flick of sail, bird on the horizon.
Hold to that? No, adjust,
adjust.

In Irons

Can't steer without headway
No headway without filled sail
No filled sail without steering off-wind
Can't steer

Who has not been clapped thus
by the wind's sardonic applause
sails flapping rudder useless

Stuck mid-passage
knowing oneself ridiculous
unable to get onto
one tack or another
while all one's fellow
competitors fizz by

Someone in honest doubt
may swither for days months years,
unable to turn to any kind of wind
tiller redundant in the hand
and all the time the current bearing
away from our goal

Thus we sat in irons off Houton Head
becalmed as the wind hustled by
till eventually one of us said

Sod this, and reached for the oar.

But it lingers doesn't it
bafflement at being
motionless amongst motion
when you wake in your own
body's boat at night
canvas heart flapping   going nowhere

In irons at the end
of your last exhale
what will you reach for

what oar will you find
to steer into whatever
if any wind blows then?

The Log *(resumed)*

It's called *working* to windward for good reason.
6 nautical miles became 12.
Hips, shoulders, legs weary of brace,
numbed by spray's sluice.
Dead Reckoning: in the gap between
where we point and where we go,
life opens its waters.

    Those lines we drew last night on the chart
held up against the gridless sea
are all too delible
       (yet work, sometimes).

So goes *pilotage*, our devotion to order
through flux of sea and weather,
    getting where we yearn
        by hard means,
that we would know it better:

 by chart, transit and surmise,
 by beam reach, broad reach, close reach,
 by close haul, tack, forced gybe,
 by Total Error and Dead Reckoning,
 line of sight and back bearing,
 by instinct and favour,
 by cold rope corroding hand,
 by Graemsay, Houton, Hoy,
 we shook out our sails without reefing.

Nosed up the Cava coast,
    failing light and swell from port
centreboard raised and home forgot -
found a channel between skerries
    dropped the main.
Jib flapping she crunched on small stones,
Crew jumped ashore with painter and anchor,
        grinning all over.

Long windward crossing,
(outboard half-cocked, dripping, silent throughout),
by sail alone we made landfall
    at twenty hundred hours

shingle under our boots yielding and dear.

IDA AND MEG.....

FOR THIRTY YEARS ALONE ON CAVA
IN PRIVATE WORSHIP THEY SANG

PRAISES OF LIFE AND LOVE

TO SHEEP AND BIRDS AND FERRY

I.W.   M.P.

ON CAVA

'Island I remember living here,
wandering beneath an empty sky'

Shelter

Shingle then bedrock then up onto turf.
Our deserted repeat deserted island
– I mean it was abandoned twice –
 exhales heather and salt in last light.

Mark makes the Whaler fast, thinking
certain announcements shake us to the keel:
overdose; landfall; with child. Checks painter
runs unsnarled through fairlead. Detail,
glory of micro-adventure!

Spray-damp breeks cling and grip, as
tent under one arm, sleeping bags
squashed in oxters, hump-backed under
food and drink, I stumble downwind
seeking shelter before dark –
              a rusty blade
         scraped back to its element,
  grey-gleaming, whetted, of use again.

    Coarse grass, tufts and hollows,
    swells, peaks – but not moving.
            I move.
    That's the difference
    between sailing and walking.

Sheep scatter, terns peep and flash, curlews
follow lament downwind.

It is the hour of flecks and blurs.
Quest for *the right place*
  is urgent, tripping, sequential,
  as though one were moving through
not an island
but a poem of an island,
as in a way one is…

   Are you gonna get that tent up?

Land dips and offers
shelter in lee of static wave.
Drop gear, hurry back, meet Mark
leaving Whaler grounded off high water,
   lurched over for the night
as falling asleep we leave the body
lying on its side.

Whisky and talk

Not home
but some new outpost of it,
cross-legged in my tent
            in dry clothes
by torchlight we wolfed
as men without women do
not a meal but *rations*.

Whisky in that context
revved across the lips then
swung round tongue's bend so smoothly
we knew ourselves re-conditioned.

That golden engine
gunned all the way down
and easeful space
opened in head and heart and hand

as we talked
as men without women do
of today's highlights
        tomorrow's resolves
            early loves and landfalls

and passing mention of fears (noted, not amplified)
        deep as the Flow itself
    as we'd sailed through so many
delusions of adequacy.

The shared doing of that day
  in tired hands lay
    acknowledged and unsaid
as the tongue finds
    on the upper lip

a late reprise of salt and whisky.

Graemsay Low

Graemsay Low's sequential flash,
behind it the glow of Stromness
where all we love now sleep -
We abandon home to locate it.
How daft is that?

And of that light
flashing on and off in the heart
whose duration and pauses
constitute its identity
there is no need to speak.

Pish

Privilege or necessity of age
  this twice or thrice nightly quitting
  warm pit for a slash in the dark?

Not that automatic
nocturnal quest to the loo and back
I woke to hear my father make,
    heavy tread past my room humming
    childlike under his breath
        Oh Jeezy-beezy loves me
        the Bible tells me so
and wondered that he went so often…

Years tell not in the mind but in the bladder.
It's a reminder
who's in charge here
as one unzips the tent and stumbles,
turf thrust wet between toes,

      to sway   stop   stand
      upright in the night
                    releasing
      streams of oneself back to earth.

I find myself
  upright in late middle-age
    a mast stuck in the ground
bracing the billowing

    spinnaker of night
as the dark hull of this island
    sails forth with constellated sails ...

Cockleshell image, I know!
   Couped by the first critical wave
but wonderful to float within
for the duration of a pish.

Damp soles dried on palms,
back in my pit,
first offices of the night performed,
I smiled at the dark and sank.

Night Beacon

the mind
a caged light
tethered to sea-bed
rocks and winks
on/off through storms

blink and gone

back again

and so on

You awake over there, pal?

Surveying Cava

We sit on the turf dyke
running along Cava like the spine
of a mottled, gutted face-down fish;
water all round, nothing hidden,
nowhere to hide - the day itself
windy, cool,
                    brightness remade.

The Flotta terminal hums,
a tractor hacks a cough on Graemsay,
lobster boat a speck off Orphir –
we can pick the machines
                    but not people.
Below the shining vacancy out there
the *Royal Oak* rests with her crew.

Sheep and birds and grass.
Four farmhouse ruins remain, plus
mangled rails, cement bases where perched once
searchlights, gun turrets, generators, canteens.
But of those world wars what's most clearly left
are giant urinals:
                    bright white porcelain
                    upright open coffins
                    albino penguins

at attention or keeled over they remain
pristine, gleaming, their surrounds long rotted –

it seems our lasting monument is not
to love, sacrifice or tragedy
                    but to the need to pee
and be occluded.

We poke among ruins.
What do you think this was for?
        Search me.
We keep our voices low, lift gently, discard,
move on and save for last
the place that matters most:
reclaimed by birds and sheep and muck,
the *Muckle House*.

Ida and Meg

(i)
Miss Woodham and Miss Peckham
known inevitably by the gossiping classes
– aka the inquisitive and mostly kind
citizens of Stromness, Houton, Orphir –
as *The Woodpeckers*
in Muckle House (not so big)
were the sole inhabitants of Cava
without company or electricity
for near-on thirty years.

They were not a couple
(all who knew them insist
as, scandalised, did they).
That is not the issue.
That does not seal the deal,
whatever they signed up to
1st April 1959 in Clevedon
when they packed everything that mattered
    (it was very little)
    (it was essential)
in a tea chest on an axle with two pram wheels,
(Ida's work, the maker and fixer)
topped by Fanny the cat in a box with a window,
Meg's peddler's licence in her purse,
attached the rope harness,
            looked at each other –

and if you want to get a handle
on a door into your life,
you could start by reaching for
whatever passed between them
– a promise, a joke, a shared
  sense of how things *shall be* –
that morning in 1959
when Meg fitted the harness across Ida's shoulders
and they took a deep breath, stepped North.

There must have been
the island they carried in their heads,
and the island they themselves invented
every unswerving step away from Clevedon.
In the Borders the pram wheel broke.
They left the bogie with a farmer's boy,
put the tea chest on a train,
picked up the cat and walked on.

How they chose to live
and what they inhabited,
their daily living by each other
with nowhere to hide,
each the other's staff,
makes marriage seem faint-hearted.

The sheer bloody work of it!
After the first 400 bags of sheep-shit, bottles,
floats and bruck carried from the House,
Meg stopped counting.

Without electricity,
peat for heat, a harmonium, books and radio,
a flower garden in one ruin, veg in another,
their lives together so long in such proximity:
  a conundrum
    a bare island
only vision and work make habitable.

Peat dug from the Calf, Meg rowed,
Ida bagged and worked the pulleys.
There was a well of sorts,
for water always seeps in Orkney
between sandstone layers; buckets lowered, yoked,
staggered to the house, till Ida rigged
a hosepipe, pump and storage tank.

Standing in the debris of their lives
among buckets, a rusted *Singer*, curtain rags,
whatever kept them bound together
(Meg slept in Muckle House,
Ida in the Wendy by the shore)
is more intriguing than desire
to one in his life's October.
It could be each had sunk

a shaft down through their days
of necessary work, bird-silence, sea,
and reached the water table, life itself,
and there lived as they wished
in *concurrence*

              subterranean.

Fractal

The shoreline of an island
one mile by a half,
when your feet have trod each tussock ,
when your hands have paused among seaweed,
hauled creels, stacked peat, sought pretty stones,
plucked mussels, lifted useful bruck and sea-glass,
is indefinitely long.
                    Attention is fractylic,
closer you look the more there is,
each fretted island
                    world without end.

They were not hermits.
Anyone who dropped in was welcome
(especially if they brought cake, mail or gin).
They rowed to Church when weather permitted,
stayed for lunch or tea, then
with a brisk wave, pushed off.
They haunt us because
the island they went back to
was anyone's life, only more so.

Harmonium

Ida rode her motorbike for peats.
Meg rowed for paraffin, calor gas, batteries and tea,
picked up mail and library books.
Ida learned violin, guitar, mandolin.
In winter evenings they read,
sang psalms or songs of their youth...

Amazing grace, how sweet the sound!
– Part trumpet, part bronchitic,
Mark pumped the poo-spattered harmonium,
mice and spiders ran crazed as
from the bottom of an Omo box,
I lift out yellowed sheet music:
'Best Devotional Songs, price 7/6',
keep for my beloved
to play upon her uke.
That saved a wretch like me...

It ends, as it must, in enforced departure
(Meg deaf, half-blind, Ida's arms arthritic
from thirty years of rowing) to twin caravans near Orphir.
Final illness and death of Meg.
Ida soldiered on, as you do, in Care.

Yea when this flesh and heart shall fail
Respectable, religious, stubborn, earthly,
how can we know the pilgrimage begun
that morning Meg harnessed Ida's shoulders,

And mortal life shall cease
what flag fluttered over their hearts
        as they slipped anchor from Clevedon,
I shall possess within the veil
creaked North by unsettled ways,
    or what they made
            here in Muckle House?
A life of joy and peace

I guess they got good at crosswords.

Life on Cava

Not a tree not a bush
Not a mast not a light
Not a road not a rabbit
Not a path

No socket no cycle
No pylon no hot tap
No voice but their own
Loud among sheep

*

A hen-house a peat stack
A tilley lamp a mandolin
A new boat an old friend
An insult forgiven

A left boot on the east shore
A right boot on the west
A series of gales and visits
A body washed up bootless

The peace after visits
The silence after gales
Love returning
That exceptional tide

An evening of music
The unacknowledged birthday
A long-awaited guest
Death of last cat

Here is love laying down oars
Here is love rubbing in liniment
Here is love calling the doctor
A toast to life passed

All that is here
All that is not
Through thirty years
Among gulls and sea

Meg and Ida centred daylight's circle
Moon's low spume-flecked arc

Improvisation

I stood at the doorless door
of that decrepit house of love
thinking Skip is a rare musician
and a radical Baptist Christian
but that is not the fret
my doubtful fingers press

And we do not talk about this

Yet when we make music
or take to the sea
we harmonise because we
agree how the tune goes
in spirit if not in detail

(he jaunty on fiddle
me clanging coarse banjo)

In heart's open sessions
all voices ring true
when friends meet to hymn
Country or Blues

A Cava grace

Opinions? Faiths?
Froth and fingernails!

This the sea

Here my hand

SMOOTH BROAD GLOSSY SNOUTS - OH MAN. DOLPHiNS

SWELL UNDER STRAKES. THESE ROLLERS LiFTED

BORE US ALOFT. AS WE TORE DOWN THE SEA-ROADS!

IT'S CALLED 'GOOSE WINGING' AND RIGHTLY. JIB WIDE TO STARBOARD, MAIN FULL PORT, TWIN DAZZLING WINGS FLEW US OVER BRING DEEPS

GMB 96

GOOSEWING
HOMEWARD

' ... He ever has longing who hastens on water'

Leaving Cava

Mark pulled the door to, secured with twine
as birds flew in and out the empty windows.
For sure, these were not ordinary folk.

We shouldered our tents, set off for the shore
where rising tide crept round the *Arctic Whaler*,
lurching up from her side.

One look back at Muckle Ruin.
The end of love is commonplace,
the voyage not.

Homewards

Top of the tide
    sea door opens
mast swings upright
    hull quivers for off

Mark hoists the jib, lets it flap.
Hand on thwart, I pass the packs,
swing tents aboard;
                braced on Cava shingle,
last push,
            scramble on as beach retreats.

Sheets tight, sail fills, rudder has its song.
We swing past skerries and away.

The boat refloated

It is wood, metal and rope
as Miss Woodham and Miss Peckham
were flesh, blood and bone,
so don't come all post-Modern
with me, mate –

   but the slap of the sea
left glaze on the glasses
we saw it all through.

That trip became myth
long before we beached,
and the boat that tacks
      on this white sea
        is not the boat
      we sailed that day

and if this craft
on its ploy capsizes
     the fault is mine
not wind or tide or sudden gust:

it would be faltering at the controls,
poor judgement, a moment's inattention,
   tired ear missing the beat,
the killer wave that coups the craft

and in that foundering
       that disbelief
skipper and all hands
  the Flow itself
would sink and drain
       down the plughole.

We pushed off at high water,
  went goose-winging briskly home
    wind and tide backing,
surfing the swell
  Skipper lounging mid-ships
    Self at the helm

my hand on juddering tiller
already starting to scribe
tree, cotton and ore
    re-launched as '*Arctic Whaler*'.

A doubtful sailor's prayer

Pray not for someone to calm these waters
That would be miracle or foul

Eyes wide open
with calm sough
hand light on the tiller

as seas flex and fissure
choose love or fear
– up to you, friend -

across the pitching world
holding what is
        in steadfast regard
to the end

Dolphins

Tide backing, wind behind,
   Crew at the tiller,
        Skip lounged for'ard
taking bearings, thinking of home.

   Swell under strakes, these rollers lifted
      smooth broad glossy snouts – oh man,
        dolphins bore us aloft
    as we tore down the sea-roads!

It's called 'goose-winging' and rightly.
Jib wide to starboard, main full port,
     twin dazzling wings
   flew us over Bring Deeps,
        banked by Clestrain, beat past Cairston…

Sun hot, fleeces unzipped, hats off,
salt dried in around our eyes,
        set wild our hair

and in our wake happiness
    grooved white in blue then evened out.

Harvest

Small talk, largesse of silence.
High on doing, we harvest
yesterday's hard work to windward.

Second harvest comes later,
seed flowing from the thresher.
Then milling, sieving, proving.

Later again
lights on in the bakery
through to dawn.

Slipway

In Hatston's lee we dithered,
wanting home, wanting to sail longer,
    never quit the life of motion
        nor cease to farm the liquid field –

tide bore us between Ness and Holms.
Waving on the slipway, all we return for.

– I mean, not only beloveds,
children, pals, decrepit dog,
but that part we stabled when we left
that awaits us now and every morn,
bright-eyed, earth-smelling –

Pick up the traces!
        The daily work horse
        sets haunches and heart
to the task.

Lubber

Wake in the night, glad lubber,
your mini-epic done,
Arctic Whaler on its cradle by the Ness.
      Yet in the inner ear
and under solid ground,
      the rocking persists.

Put down your pen, Skip. Sign off the Log.

Post script
(i.m. George Mackay Brown)

April 1996: brisk day
waves flecked to the horizon
so bright so bright

His last murmur
in the Balfour Hospital, Kirkwall
'I see hundreds of ships leaving harbour'

   Trust a poet
    to hoard a good last line
    then toss it overboard

    marker buoy
    as the faithful bilge pump
    slows   sputters   stops

Every lover, parent, friend
at the end sails away
from we who harboured them

Yet he willed
a craft so well made
he could sink on an even keel

as waters poured in
through Orkney's harbouring arms

Epigraphs from:

page 7
CANTO I, EZRA POUND

page 35
ROBIN WILLIAMSON *Maya*

page 59
from the Anglo Saxon poem
The Seafarer, trans. Jonathan A.
Glenn

'FOUND AT SEA' ANDREW GREIG